Blue eyes, black hair,
Brown eyes, brown hair,
Look at all the colours everywhere.
Lots of different children,
Lots of different families,
Living in a world we share.

A DORLING KINDERSLEY BOOK

Illustrations by Lisa Flather
Photography by Philip Dowell, Jo Foord,
Steve Gorton, Dave King, Stephen Oliver,
Roger Phillips, Susanna Price,
Steve Shott, Harry Taylor

With special thanks to Fisty Read
and Amanda Cernish

First published in Great Britain in 1996
by Dorling Kindersley Limited,
9 Henrietta Street, London WC2E 8PS

The publisher would like to thank the following
agencies and photographers for their kind
permission to reproduce their photographs:
(t=top, b=bottom, c=centre, l=left, r=right)

Bruce Coleman Ltd.: 13br; Galaxy Picture
Library/Robin Scagell: 13tc; The Image Bank: 13cl;
Tony Stone Worldwide/Michael Busselle: 13tl;
Tony Craddock: 13c; Pascal Crapet: 13cr;
Manfred Mehling: 13bl; Oliver Strewe: 13bc;
Pictor International: 13tr

A CIP catalogue record for this book is
available from the British Library

ISBN 0-7513-5343-4

Colour reproduction by Colourscan
Printed in Italy by L.E.G.O.

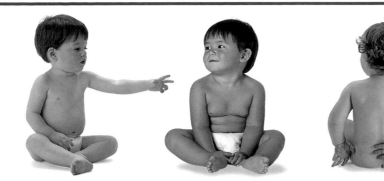

BABY'S BOOK OF
THE BODY

Roger Priddy

DORLING KINDERSLEY
LONDON • NEW YORK • STUTTGART

My body

hair

head

arm

knee

Every part
of my body
has a special
name and
a different
job to do.

shoulder

leg

finger

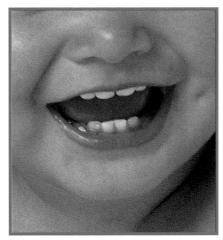

I eat with
my **mouth**.

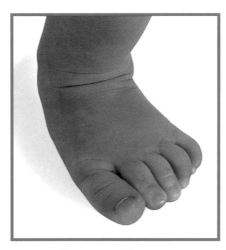

I stand on
my **feet**.

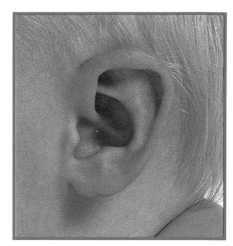

I hear with
my **ears**.

I look at things
with my **eyes**.

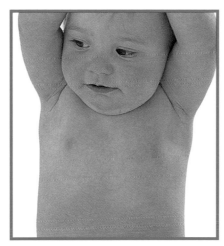

My **chest** moves
as I breathe.

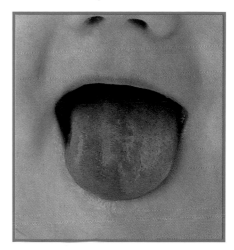

I can taste with
my **tongue**.

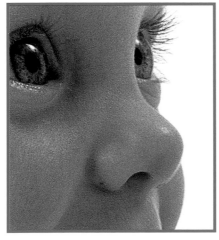

I smell with
my **nose**.

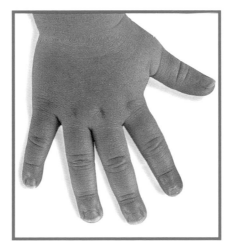

I use my **hands**
to pick things up.

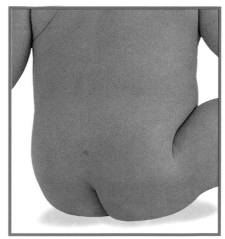

I sit on
my **bottom**.

Look at me

We all have two eyes, a nose, and a mouth,
but no one looks the same as anyone else.

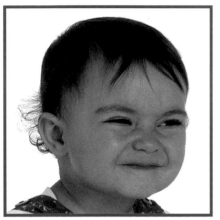  

What colour is your hair? Is it curly or is it straight?

  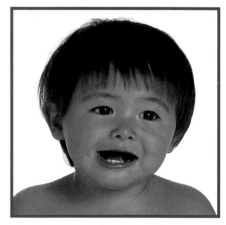

What colour is your skin? Can you count how many teeth you have?

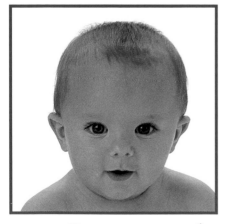  

Can you touch all the parts of your face and name them?

Making faces

When we feel happy, we smile and laugh.
Can you tell how these babies are feeling?

amazed

thoughtful

excited

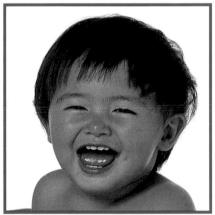

happy

worried

upset

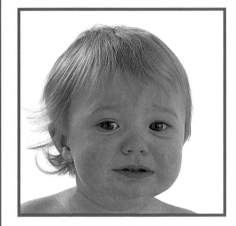

sad

surprised

puzzled

How many?

1 chubby bottom

2 wide eyes

3 friendly faces

4 wobbly legs

5 wriggly toes

10 little fingers

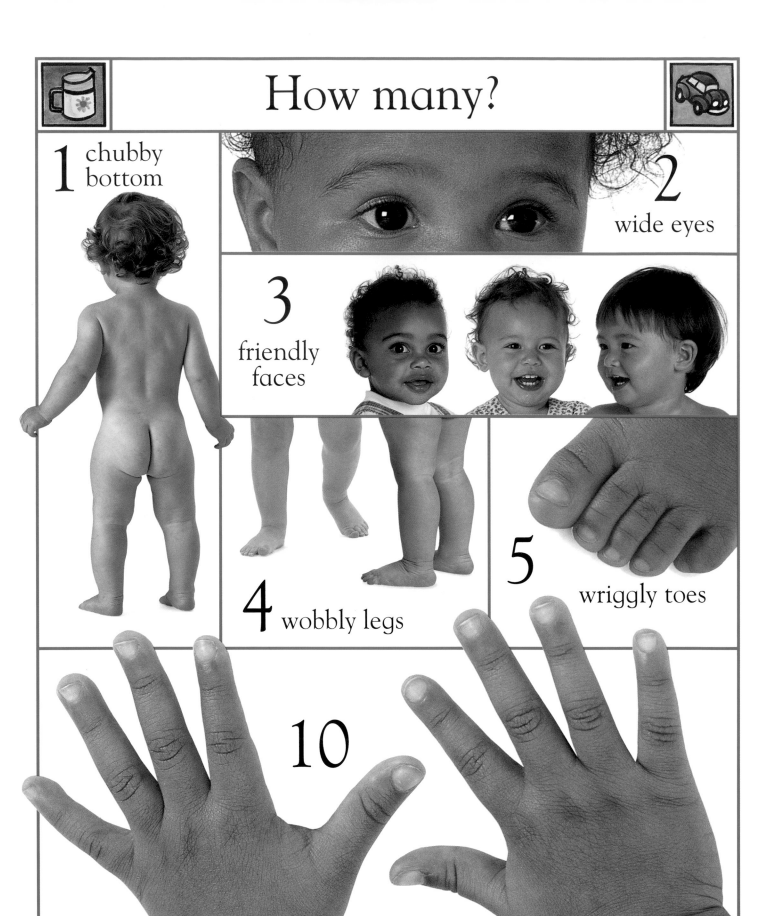

You can count on us

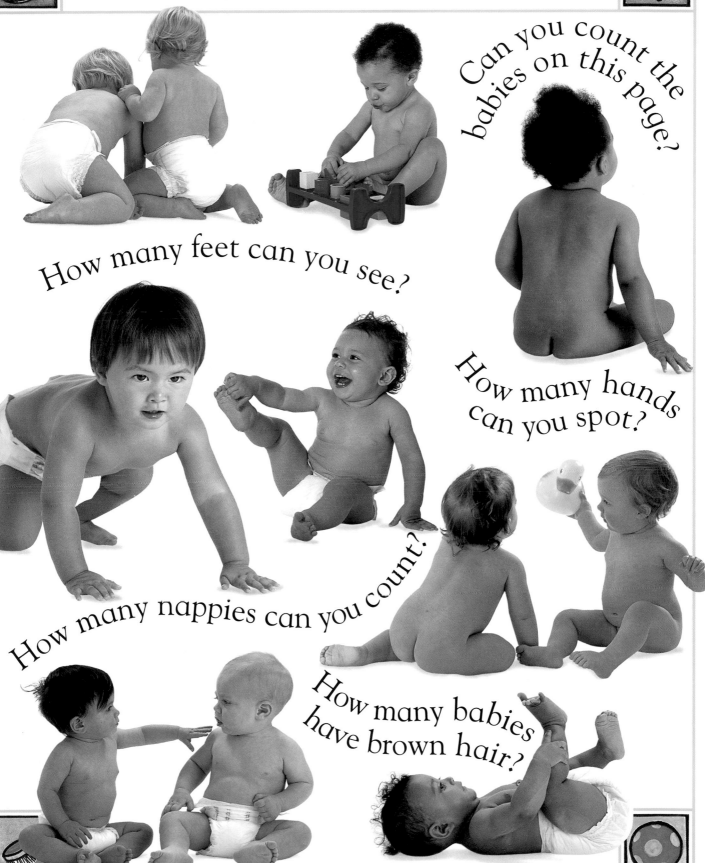

Can you count the babies on this page?

How many feet can you see?

How many hands can you spot?

How many nappies can you count?

How many babies have brown hair?

Things to see

The world is full of things to see, at home and outside. Can you name them?

spoon

bib

dog

cat

teddy

rattle

cup

sheep standing
under a green **tree**

a **street** at night
with twinkling **lights**

fluffy **clouds**
in a blue **sky**

white **sand** on a
tropical **beach**

cows munching in
grassy, green **fields**

a **city** full of
tall buildings

the **sun** setting in
an orange **sky**

snowy **mountains**
covered in **clouds**

yellow **sunflowers**
facing the **sun**

What's that noise?

bang

bang

bang
bang
bang

bang drum

spinning top

hummmm

hummm

hummmm

hummm

rattle

tch-tch tch-tch tch-tch

sneeze

achoOOO

bee

bzzzzz

bzzz

bzzzzzzzzz

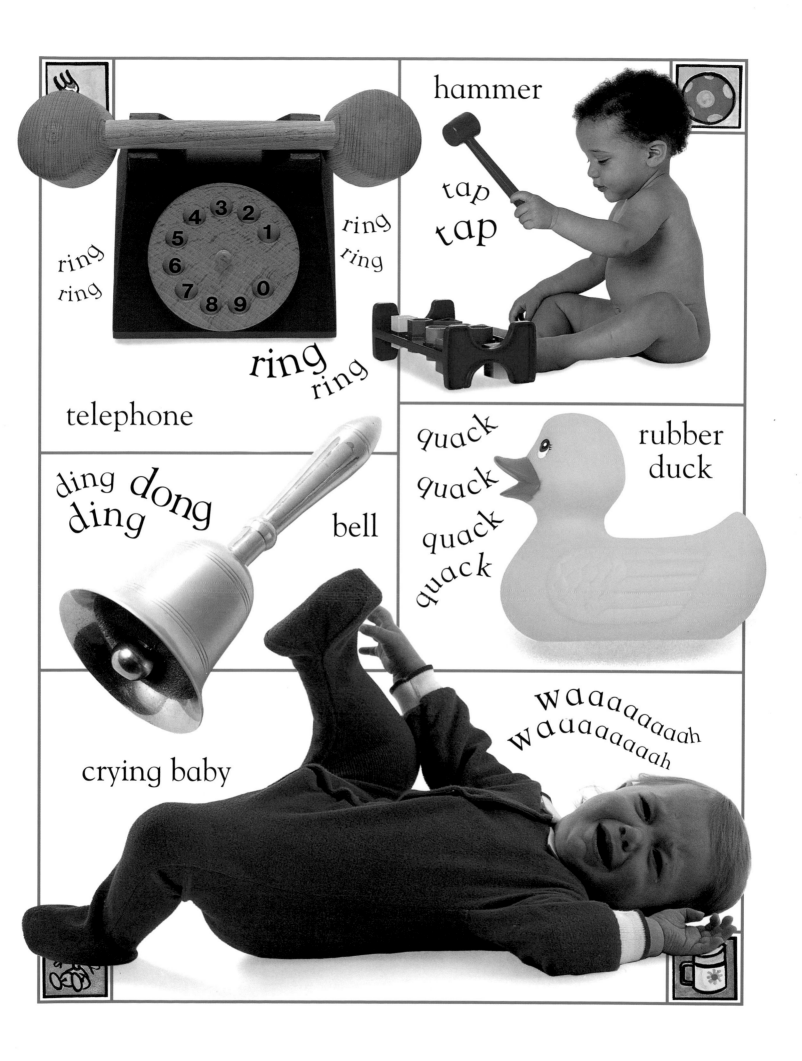

telephone

ring ring ring ring ring ring ring

hammer

tap tap

bell

ding dong ding

quack quack quack quack

rubber duck

crying baby

waaaaaaah waaaaaaah

Things to do

giving

hiding

picking things up

playing games

crawling along

sucking
a thumb

pointing
a finger

carrying
a chair

having a drink

clapping
hands

Things to eat

We all love eating food, but it is fun
to see, smell, touch, and even hear it, too.

soft, green grapes, huddle in a bunch

the dimply peel of a sweet
smelling, juicy, round orange

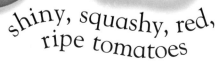

shiny, squashy, red,
ripe tomatoes

a prickly, patterned
pineapple wearing
a spiky, green hat

crunchy, munchy, round, green apple

squishy raspberries melt in your mouth

unzip a bendy, yellow banana

crusty bread outside, soft and fluffy inside

knobbly potatoes

bumpy broccoli, like a little tree

a sharp, smelly onion makes your eyes water

still in their jackets

tiny, shiny peas are snug in their pod

Mix and match

Can you match us with the things
on the opposite page?

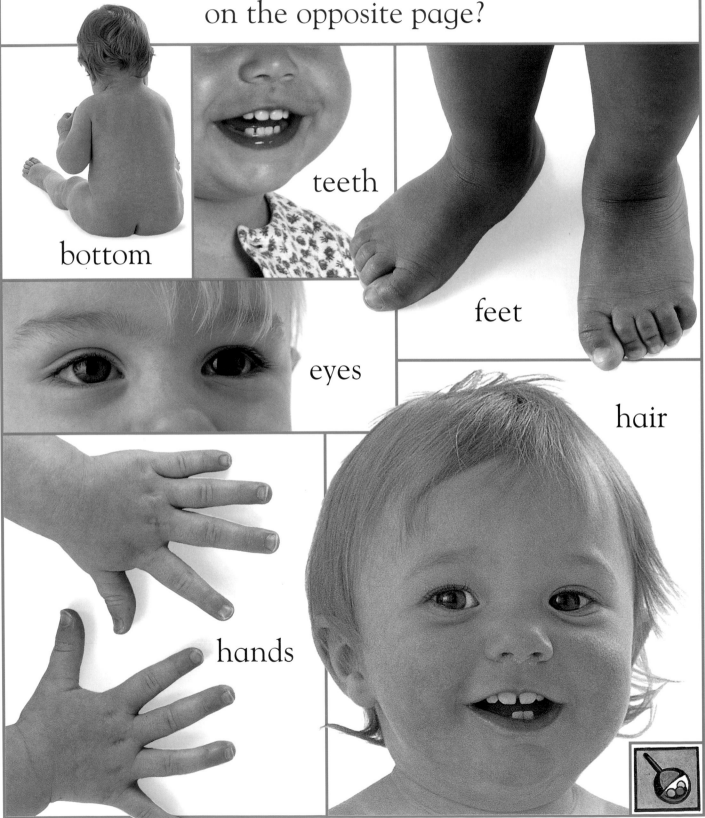

bottom

teeth

feet

eyes

hair

hands

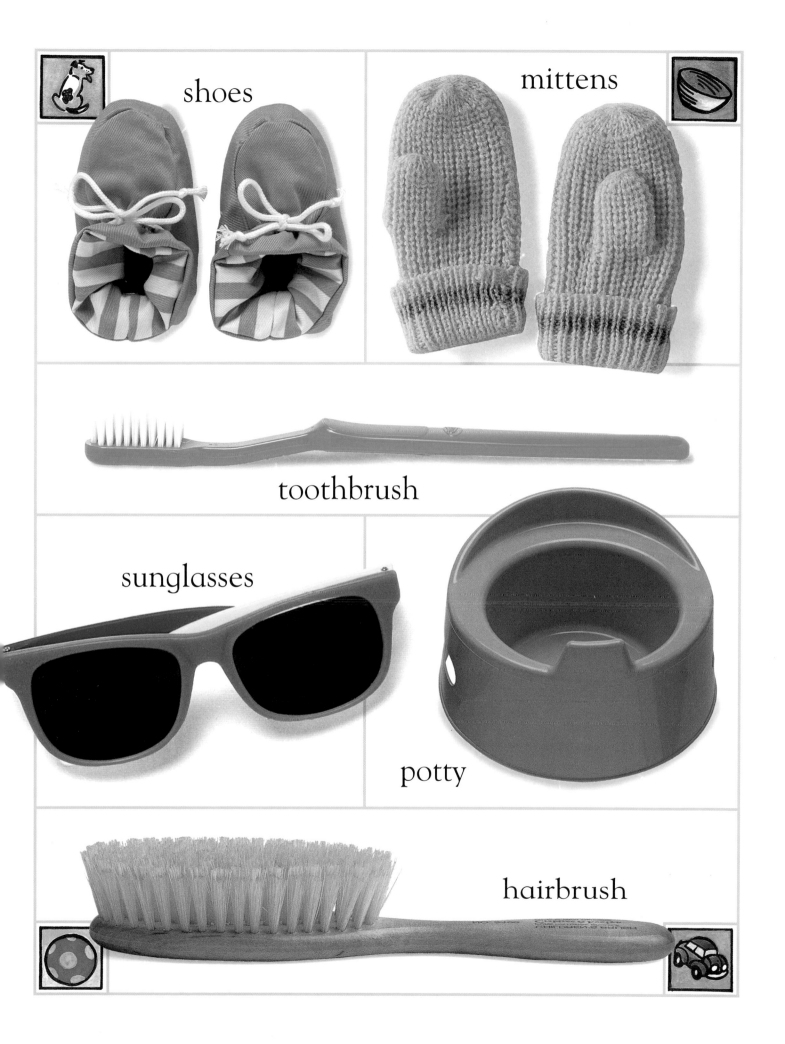

shoes

mittens

toothbrush

sunglasses

potty

hairbrush